Mary Jones, Diane Fellowes-Freeman and ...

Cambridge Checkpoint

Science

Skills Builder Workbook

8

CAMBRIDGE
UNIVERSITY PRESS

CAMBRIDGE
UNIVERSITY PRESS

University Printing House, Cambridge CB2 8BS, United Kingdom

One Liberty Plaza, 20th Floor, New York, NY 10006, USA

477 Williamstown Road, Port Melbourne, VIC 3207, Australia

314–321, 3rd Floor, Plot 3, Splendor Forum, Jasola District Centre, New Delhi – 110025, India

79 Anson Road, #06–04/06, Singapore 079906

Cambridge University Press is part of the University of Cambridge.

It furthers the University's mission by disseminating knowledge in the pursuit of education, learning and research at the highest international levels of excellence.

www.cambridge.org
Information on this title: www.cambridge.org/9781316637203 (Paperback)

© Cambridge University Press 2017

First published 2017

20 19 18 17 16 15 14 13 12 11 10 9 8

Printed in India by Multivista Global Pvt Ltd

A catalogue record for this publication is available from the British Library

ISBN 978-1-316-63720-3 Paperback

Produced for Cambridge University Press by White-Thomson Publishing
www.wtpub.co.uk
Editor: Izzi Howell
Designer: Clare Nicholas

All Checkpoint-style questions and sample answers within this workbook are written by the authors.

Acknowledgements

The authors and publishers acknowledge the following sources for photographs:

Cover Pal Hermansen/Steve Bloom Images/Alamy Stock Photo

....

Contents

Introduction

Welcome to the Cambridge Checkpoint Science Skills Builder Workbook 8

The Cambridge Checkpoint Science course covers the Cambridge Secondary 1 Science curriculum framework. The course is divided into three stages: 7, 8 and 9.

You should use this Skills Builder Workbook with Coursebook 8 and Workbook 8. This workbook does not cover all of the curriculum framework at stage 8; instead it gives you extra practice in key topics, focusing on those that are the most important, to improve your understanding and confidence.

The tasks will help you with scientific enquiry skills, such as planning investigations, drawing tables to record your results, and plotting graphs.

The workbook will also help you to use your knowledge to work out the answers to new questions.

As you work through the tasks in this Skills Builder Workbook you should find that you get better at these skills.

You could then try to complete some of the exercises in the Checkpoint Science Workbook.

If you get stuck with a task:

Read the question again and look carefully at any diagrams, to find any clues.

Look up any words you do not understand in the glossary at back of the Checkpoint Science Coursebook, or in your dictionary.

Read through the matching section in the Coursebook. Look carefully at the diagrams there too.

Check the reference section at the back of the Coursebook. There is a lot of useful information there.

Introducing the learners

Nor   Amal   Sam

Anna   Elsa   Jon

1.1 Photosynthesis

This exercise relates to **1.2 Leaves** from the Coursebook.

> In this exercise, you think about what plants need, and what they make, when they photosynthesise.

The diagram shows a plant.

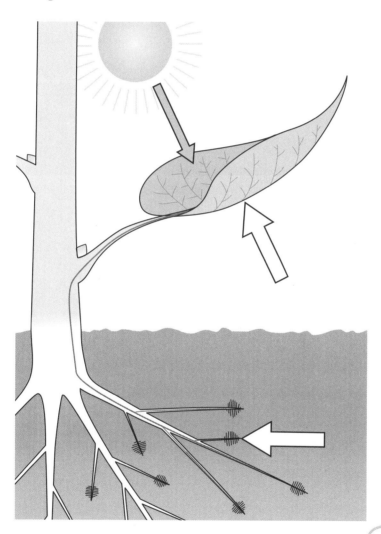

1 On the diagram, draw a label line to the part of the plant where photosynthesis happens.

Colour this part green.

Label this part with its name.

Remember

Draw your label line with a ruler.

The label line can be at any angle, but the writing should be horizontal.

2 What do plants need for photosynthesis?
Tick **three** boxes.

biomass ☐

carbon dioxide ☐

energy from light ☐

oxygen ☐

water ☐

3 What do plants make in photosynthesis?
Tick **two** boxes.

biomass ☐

carbon dioxide ☐

energy from light ☐

oxygen ☐

water ☐

4 Decide which arrow on the diagram shows how water enters the plant.

Colour this arrow blue.

Label the arrow.

5 Decide which arrow on the diagram shows how carbon dioxide enters the plant.

Colour this arrow brown.

Label the arrow.

6 Complete this sentence, using your own words.

Photosynthesis is ....

....

....

1.2 How light level affects photosynthesis

This exercise relates to **1.3 Investigating photosynthesis** from the Coursebook.

> In this exercise, you decide which variables to control in an experiment. You put results into a table and make a conclusion.

Amal does an experiment to investigate whether plants photosynthesise faster when they have more light.

The diagram shows the apparatus he uses.

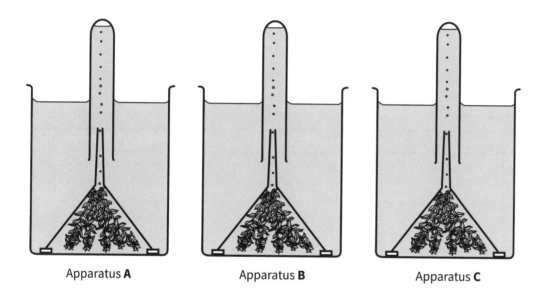

| Apparatus **A** | Apparatus **B** | Apparatus **C** |

Amal puts Apparatus **A** next to a window.

He puts Apparatus **B** in a shady corner of the same room.

He puts Apparatus **C** in a dark cupboard.

1 What should Amal keep the same for all three sets of apparatus?
Tick **three** boxes.

the amount of light ☐

the type of plant ☐

the mass of the plant ☐

the number of bubbles ☐

the temperature ☐

Amal leaves his three sets of apparatus for two days. Then he measures the volume of gas collected in each test tube.

This is what he writes down.

A $18.3 cm^3$

B $7.2 cm^3$

C $0.5 cm^3$

2 Complete Amal's results table.

Apparatus	Amount of light	
A		
B		
C		

3 What **conclusion** can Amal make from his results?
Tick **one** box.

Plants need chlorophyll for photosynthesis. ☐

Plants that live in water photosynthesise more slowly than plants that live on land. ☐

Plants photosynthesise faster when they have more light. ☐

Plants use water for photosynthesis. ☐

1.3 Water movement and temperature

This exercise relates to **1.5 Transporting water and minerals** from the Coursebook.

> In this exercise, you use a set of results to construct a line graph. You use your graph to make a conclusion.

Anna is investigating the rate of water movement up a celery stalk. She wants to find out how the temperature of the water affects this.

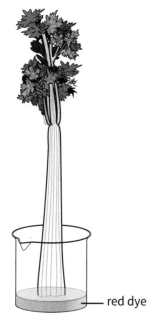

red dye

She takes eight celery stalks.

She stands each stalk in a beaker containing a red dye.

She puts each beaker into a water bath. Each water bath is kept at a different temperature.

After ten minutes, she takes out all of the celery stalks.

She cuts each stalk across, every 0.5 cm along.

She looks for the red dye in the slices of the stalk.

Anna records how far the dye has travelled up each stalk. She writes her results in a table.

Anna's results table:

Temperature in °C	Distance the dye travels in cm
0	1.0
10	1.9
20	3.1
30	4.0
40	4.8
50	3.2
60	7.0
70	8.1

1 Which one of Anna's results does not fit the pattern?

Draw a circle around it in the table.

2 Use Anna's results to construct a line graph on the grid on the next page.

Put **temperature in °C** on the x-axis.

Put **distance the dye travels in cm** on the y-axis.

Draw a **line of best fit**.

3 What **conclusion** can Anna make from her experiment?
Tick **one** box.

Plants need more water when the temperature is higher. ☐

As temperature increases, the rate of transport of water in celery stalks increases. ☐

Celery leaves use water for photosynthesis. ☐

Remember

Make sure that your scale goes up in equal steps.

Plot each point with a small, neat cross.

When you draw the line of best fit, ignore the result that you drew a circle around in the table.

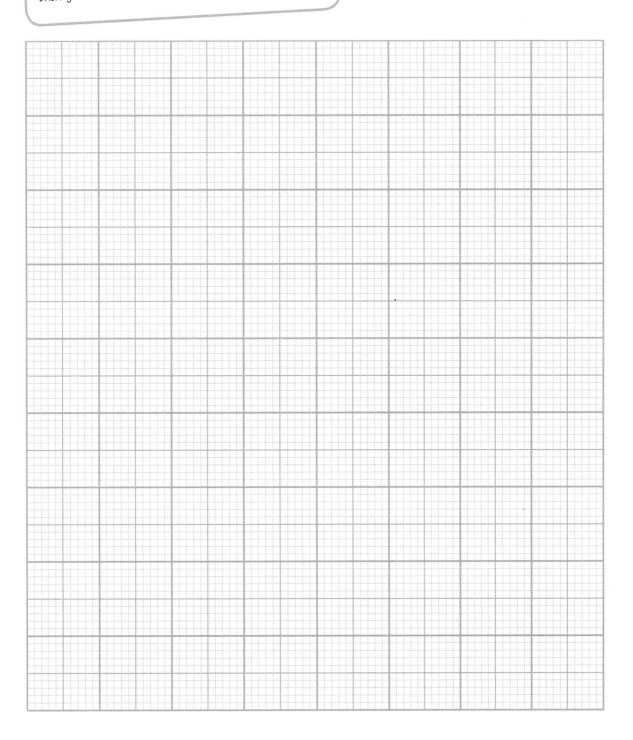

2.1 Food test results

This exercise relates to **2.1 Nutrients** from the Coursebook.

> In this exercise, you use your knowledge of food tests to complete a results table and make conclusions.

Sam and Jon test different foods for starch and sugar.

The pictures below show the apparatus that they use for the two tests.

Apparatus **A**   Apparatus **B**

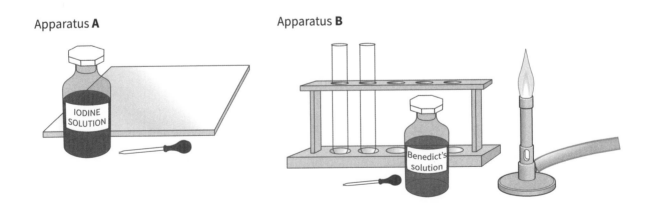

1 Which nutrient does Apparatus **A** test for?

....

2 Describe how Sam and Jon use Apparatus **A**.

....

....

....

3 What colour is iodine solution?

....

> **Remember**
>
> Look at your Coursebook if you are not sure. You can find information about food tests in section 2.1.

4 What colour do you see if the iodine test is positive?

....

5 Which nutrient does Apparatus **B** test for?

....

6 Describe how Sam and Jon use Apparatus **B**.

....

....

....

7 What colour is Benedict's solution?

....

8 What colour do you see if the Benedict's test is positive?

....

Here are some of the results that Sam and Jon write down.

steamed rice - blue-black with iodine solution, blue with Benedict's

chicken - orange-brown with iodine solution, blue with Benedict's

sweet bun - blue-black with iodine solution, brick red with Benedict's

lemonade - orange-brown with iodine solution, brick red with Benedict's

9 Use Sam's and Jon's results to complete the results chart.

Food	Colour after testing with iodine solution	Colour after testing with Benedict's solution	Conclusion

2.2 Analysing information about nutrients

This exercise relates to **2.2 A balanced diet** from the Coursebook.

In this exercise, you find information in a table to help you to answer questions.

The table shows some of the nutrients contained in 100 g of different foods.

Food	Protein in g	Fat in g	Carbohydrate in g	Calcium in mg	Vitamin C in mg
brazil nuts	12	60	4	180	0
chapatis	8	13	50	70	0
chicken	29	7	0	0	0
coconut	3	36	4	2	0
fish	18	3	0	0	0
milk	3	4	5	120	1
orange	1	9	9	40	50
tomatoes	1	0	3	0	20

1 Which food contains the most protein?

....

2 Which food contains the most vitamin C?

....

3 How much fat is there in 200 g of milk?

.........g

Remember

Read the sentence above the table carefully.

Elsa and Nor discuss the information in the table.

Brazil nuts contain more calcium than all the other nutrients put together.

Brazil nuts contain more fat than all the other nutrients put together.

Remember

Look carefully at the headings in the table.

There are 1000 mg in 1 g.

4 Who is right – Elsa or Nor?

Explain your answer.

....

....

....

5 Which food would be best for a child who has weak teeth and bones? Explain your answer.

Food: ....

Explanation: ....

....

....

2.3 Digesting starch using amylase

This exercise relates to **2.6 Enzymes** from the Coursebook.

> In this exercise, you think about how to do an experiment using amylase and starch. You also explain a set of results.

Amylase is an enzyme. It breaks big starch molecules into small sugar molecules.

Amal does an experiment using amylase and starch.

He puts some starch solution into two test tubes.

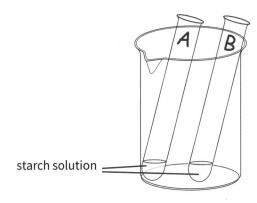

Amal dips a glass rod into the starch solution.

Then he dips the glass rod into a drop of iodine solution on a white tile.

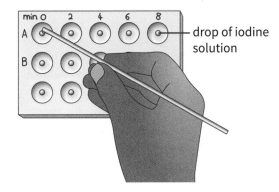

1 The drop of iodine solution went blue-black. Why did this happen?

....

Amal adds some amylase solution to test tube **A**. He adds an equal volume of water to test tube **B**.

Every two minutes, he tests the contents of the test tubes to see if they contain starch. He cleans the glass rod after every test.

2 Why must Amal clean the glass rod after every test?

....

....

The diagram shows the tile after Amal has done all the tests.

The diagram shows that the drop of iodine does **not** go blue-black when a sample from tube **A** is added at six minutes.

3 Why does this happen?
Tick **one** box.

The amylase has broken down all of the starch in tube **A**. ☐

The starch has broken down all of the amylase in tube **A**. ☐

The iodine solution has all been broken down. ☐

4 Explain why the samples from tube **B** still turn the drops of iodine blue-black after eight minutes.

....

....

Amal decides to do another experiment with amylase and starch.

5 Which of these questions can Amal investigate by doing an experiment in his school laboratory?

Does amylase work faster at 40 °C than at 20 °C? ☐

Are amylase molecules a different shape than starch molecules? ☐

Explain your answer.

....

....

....

3.1 Parts of the circulatory system

This exercise relates to **3.1 The human circulatory system** from the Coursebook.

> In this exercise, you decide which part of the circulatory system matches a description.

These are names of different parts of the circulatory system:

artery   **blood**   **blood vessel**   **heart**   **vein**

1 Write the name of each part next to its description.

  a This organ pumps blood all around the circulatory system. ....

  b This is a tube that carries blood around the body. ....

  c This is a liquid that transports different substances around the body. ....

  d This type of blood vessel carries blood away from the heart. ....

  e This type of blood vessel carries blood towards the heart. ....

2 Three of these statements are true and three are false.
   Tick the **three** true statements.

Blood picks up oxygen in the lungs. ☐

All arteries contain oxygenated blood. ☐

Blood travels from the left side of the heart to the lungs. ☐

All arteries carry blood away from the heart. ☐

Oxygenated blood and deoxygenated blood mix together inside the heart. ☐

Oxygen enters and leaves the blood by diffusion. ☐

3.2 Investigating pulse rate

This exercise relates to **3.2 The heart** from the Coursebook.

> In this exercise, you plan an experiment on pulse rate. You decide
> which variables need to be changed, controlled and measured.

Jon and Sam want to know
if a person's pulse rate is
affected by their age.

They make a list of 20 people
they know, with different
ages from 3 years old to
80 years old.

They measure the pulse rate
for each person.

1 What is the variable that Jon and Sam must **change** in their experiment?
Tick **one** box.

the person's age ☐

the pulse rate ☐

the time of day ☐

whether the person is resting or exercising ☐

2 What is the variable that Jon and Sam must **measure** in their experiment?
Tick **one** box.

the person's age ☐

the pulse rate ☐

the time of day ☐

whether the person is resting or exercising ☐

3 Which variables must Jon and Sam **keep the same** in their experiment?
Tick **two** boxes.

the person's age ☐

the pulse rate ☐

the time of day ☐

whether the person is resting or exercising ☐

Afterwards, the boys discuss how they can improve their experiment.

We should find three people for each age, so we have three readings for each age.

We should ask everyone to sit still for ten minutes before we measure their pulse rate.

4 Explain why Sam's idea is good.

....

....

....

5 Explain why Jon's idea is good.

....

....

....

4.1 Measuring lung volumes

This exercise relates to **4.1 The human respiratory system** from the Coursebook.

> In this exercise, you complete a results table, calculate mean values and draw a bar chart.

Nor and Anna want to know if students who play wind instruments in the school orchestra can push more air out of their lungs than students who play stringed instruments.

The girls take a large, empty bottle. They mark a scale on the side to show volumes.

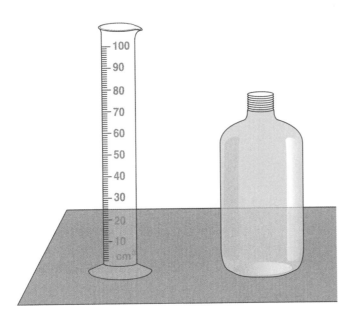

1 Describe how Nor and Anna can make the scale on the bottle.

....

....

....

Nor and Anna fill the bottle with water. They turn the full
bottle upside down, with its open top in a large container of water.

Amal plays a wind instrument.
The girls ask Amal to blow into the
bottle as hard as he can. They use
the scale to record how much water
Amal can push out of the bottle.

Then they test eight other
musicians.

Here are the results that
Nor and Anna collect.

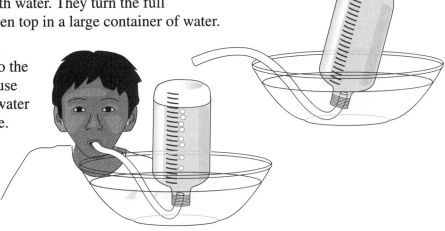

boys who play wind instruments: 2100 cm³   1965 cm³   2005 cm³

girls who play wind instruments: 1950 cm³

boys who play stringed instruments: 1865 cm³   1950 cm³

girls who play stringed instruments: 1905 cm³   1910 cm³   1885 cm³

2 Complete Nor's and Anna's results table.

Person	Boy or girl	Wind or string player	Volume displaced in cm³
1	boy	wind	2100

3 Calculate the **mean** volume displaced (pushed out) for the boys who play wind instruments.

Show your working.

> **Remember**
>
> To calculate the mean of three values, add up the three values and divide by 3.

.... cm^3

4 Calculate the mean volume displaced for the boys who play stringed instruments.

Show your working.

.... cm^3

5 Calculate the mean volume displaced for the girls who play stringed instruments.

Show your working.

.... cm^3

6 Complete the **bar chart** to show Nor's and Anna's results.

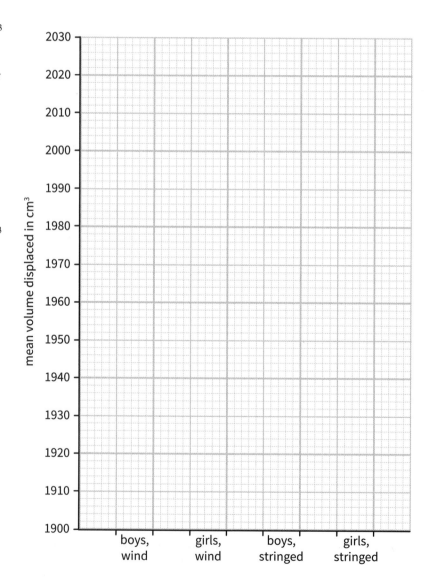

4.2 Looking at data on lung volumes

This exercise relates to **4.1 The human respiratory system** from the Coursebook.

In this exercise, you look for patterns in data.
Then you think about how to improve an experiment.

Nor and Anna did an experiment to find out if students who play wind instruments can push more air out of their lungs than students who play stringed instruments.

Their experiment is described in exercise 4.1.

Look again at the method, the results and your bar chart from exercise 4.1 to answer the questions below.

Nor and Anna discuss what their results show.

I think our results show that boys can push out larger volumes of air than girls.

I think our results show that people who play wind instruments can push out larger volumes of air than people who play stringed instruments.

1 Is Nor right? .... Explain your answer. ....

    ....

2 Is Anna right? .... Explain your answer. ....

    ....

3 Nor's and Anna's teacher says that the girls cannot make any definite conclusions from their results.

    He asks them to try to improve their experiment.

    What will improve the girls' experiment?
    Tick **two** boxes.

    Collecting more results from more people in the orchestra. ☐

    Finding out whether playing a percussion instrument affects lung volume. ☐

    Making three measurements for each person. ☐

    Measuring how fast each person can run. ☐

4.3 Respiration by yeast

This exercise relates to **4.3 Aerobic respiration** from the Coursebook.

> In this exercise, you think about how to choose apparatus, and the correct way to use a thermometer. You make a prediction about temperature change.

Elsa wants to find out what happens to the temperature when yeast respires.

She has some yeast mixed with water. She measures $25\,cm^3$ of it and puts it into an insulated cup.

Then she adds $25\,cm^3$ of sugar solution.

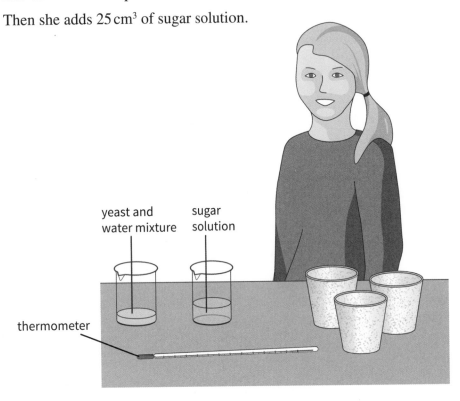

1   One piece of apparatus that Elsa needs is missing from the diagram.

    State what this apparatus is, and why Elsa needs it.

    ....

    ....

    ....

2 Elsa measures the temperature of the mixture of yeast and sugar solution in the cup.

How should Elsa measure the temperature?
Tick **all** correct statements.

Hold the thermometer in the liquid and then take it out to read it carefully. ☐

Stand the thermometer in the cup so it is resting on the bottom. ☐

Hold the thermometer in the liquid and stir gently. ☐

Make sure her eyes are level with the meniscus to read the temperature. ☐

> **Remember**
>
> The meniscus is at the surface of the liquid inside the thermometer.

3 **Predict** what will happen to the temperature of the mixture in the cup.

Explain your prediction.

Prediction ....

Explanation ....

....

4 Elsa has missed out something very important from her experiment.

What has she missed out?

....

....

....

> **Remember**
>
> Look at what Elsa was trying to find out.
>
> Think about what she needs to do to be sure any temperature change she measures is due only to the yeast respiring.

5.1 Comparing egg cells and sperm cells

This exercise relates to **5.1 Gametes** from the Coursebook.

> In this exercise, you use information from a diagram to complete a comparison table about the structure of egg cells and sperm cells. Don't worry – you don't need to remember the structure of these cells!

Egg cells and sperm cells are gametes. The diagrams show an egg cell and a sperm cell.

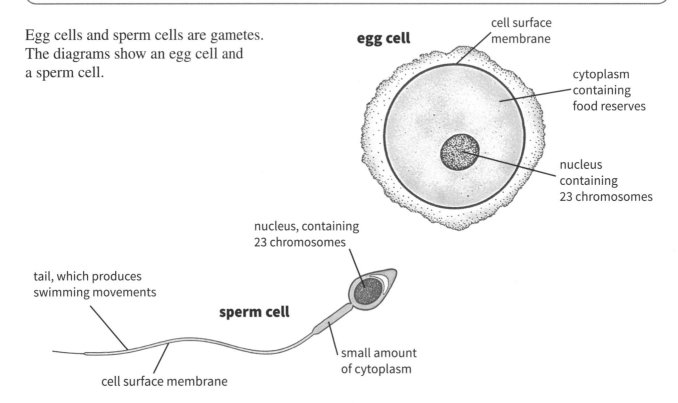

1 Complete the table on the next page to compare the structures of these two gametes. Use the labels on the diagrams to find information to write in the table. One comparison has been made for you.

2 Fertilisation happens when the nucleus of a sperm cell joins with the nucleus of an egg cell.

   Choose **one** of the differences you have written in the table.

   Suggest how this difference helps the sperm cell or the egg cell to carry out its function.

   ....

   ....

   ....

Egg cell	Sperm cell
has food reserves in the cytoplasm	does not have food reserves in the cytoplasm

Remember

Write comparable points opposite each other.

Use a ruler to draw a line underneath each pair of points.

Remember to include similarities as well as differences.

5.2 Interpreting data about smoking

This exercise relates to **5.6 Lifestyle and health** from the Coursebook.

> In this exercise, you find information in a bar chart. You use the information to answer questions about how smoking cigarettes affects a person's risk of death.

The bar chart shows information about people who died from four types of disease in a European country.

The bars show the deaths caused by smoking cigarettes, as a percentage of all deaths from that disease.

There are separate bars for men and women.

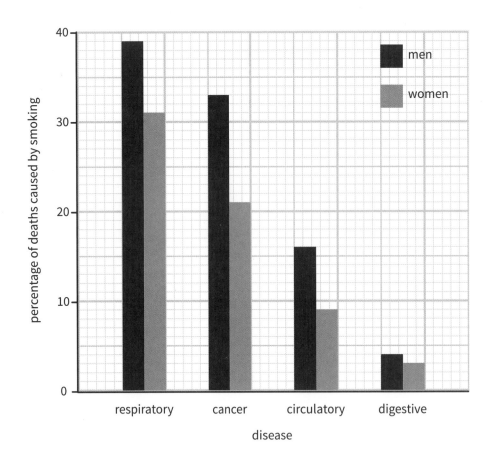

1 For which type of disease can we say:

    a death was **most** likely to be caused by smoking? ....

    b death was **least** likely to be caused by smoking? ....

2 What percentage of deaths from respiratory disease in men was caused by smoking?

   ………………………………

3 For every 200 men who died from respiratory disease, how many deaths were caused by smoking?

   ………………………………

4 What percentage of deaths from cancer in women was caused by smoking?

   ………………………………

5 For every 500 women who died from cancer, how many deaths were caused by smoking?

   ………………………………

6 Look at the percentages of deaths due to smoking for men and women, shown by the whole bar chart.

   Draw a circle around **three** words to make this a correct comparison:

   The bar chart shows that the percentages of deaths due to smoking were

   greater / smaller for **men / women** than for **men / women**.

7 Suggest an explanation for the difference stated in question 6.

   ………………………………………………………………………………………………………

   ………………………………………………………………………………………………………

   ………………………………………………………………………………………………………

Unit 6 States of matter

6.1 Change of state

This exercise relates to **6.1 Particle theory** from the Coursebook.

> In this exercise, you explain what happens when a liquid and a solid change state.

Diagram **A** shows the particles in a liquid.

A: Particles in a liquid

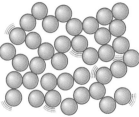

1 Complete this sentence:

If the particles in diagram **A** lose enough energy, the liquid will change

state and become a ………………………… .

2 In box **B**, draw the particles after this change of state. Complete the heading.

B: Particles in a …………………………   **C**: Particles in a …………………………

3 Complete this sentence:

If the particles in diagram **A** gain enough energy, the liquid will change state

and become a ………………………… .

4 In box **C**, draw the particles after this change of state. Complete the heading.

5 Draw a circle around the correct word or words in these sentences.

> For a solid to melt the particles must **gain / lose** energy.
>
> The particles vibrate **more / less**.
>
> The particles have enough energy to escape the **strong / weak** forces holding them in their places.
>
> The particles can now move **past / away from** each other.
>
> The solid has changed state and become a **liquid / gas**.

6 Write one of these words in each of the spaces on the diagram to name the change taking place.

melting   **freezing**   **condensing**   **boiling**

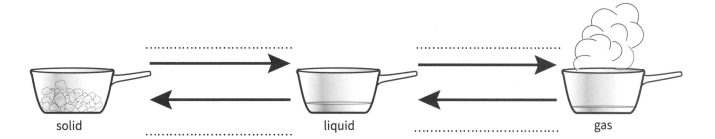

solid   liquid   gas

6.2 Investigating diffusion in the air

This exercise relates to **6.3 Investigating diffusion** from the Coursebook.

> In this exercise, you make predictions and discuss an investigation.

Some students want to investigate how quickly perfume spreads around a room.

The windows are closed.

Sam sits at the front of the classroom. He has his ears covered and he faces the front.

Amal and Elsa are at the back of the room.

This is what they do:

- Amal sprays the perfume for one second.

- Elsa starts the stopwatch.

- When Sam can smell the perfume, he raises his arm.

- Elsa stops the stopwatch.

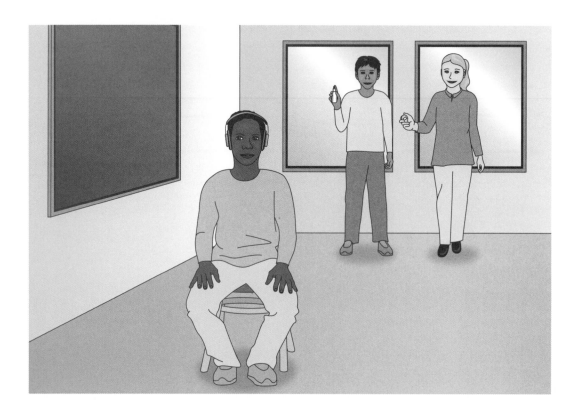

1 Why is it important that Sam does **not** see or hear when Amal sprays the perfume?

....

....

> **Remember**
>
> The particles in gas can move away from each other.
>
> Think about what speeds up the movement.

2 How does the smell reach Sam?

....

3 The students later carry out the same investigation in a **smaller** classroom.

   Will it take **more time** or **less time** for Sam to smell the perfume?

   ....

   Explain your answer.

   ....

   ....

4 When they do the investigation in the smaller classroom, should the windows be **open** or **closed**?

   ....

   Explain your answer.

   ....

   ....

5 The students do the investigation in the first classroom again, on a different day when it is much colder.

   Will it take **more time** or **less time** for Sam to smell the perfume?

   ....

   Explain your answer.

   ....

   ....

6.3 Investigating diffusion in a liquid

This exercise relates to **6.3 Investigating diffusion** from the Coursebook.

> In this exercise, you identify variables and plot a graph.

Jon and Anna are investigating how temperature affects the diffusion of food dye in water. They predict that:

The hotter the water, the faster the dye will diffuse.

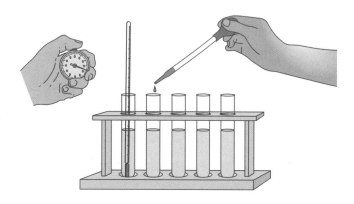

This is what they do:

- They measure the temperature of the water.

- Anna places a drop of dye in it.

- Jon times how long it takes for the dye to diffuse throughout the liquid.

1 Which variables do they need to **keep the same** in this investigation?

Give at least **two**.

....

....

....

....

Here are their results.

Temperature of water in °C	Time taken for dye to diffuse throughout the liquid in seconds
20	62
30	43
40	31
50	21
60	16

2 Plot a graph of the results. Put the **temperature** along the *x*-axis and **time** along the *y*-axis.

Draw a **curve of best fit**.

Remember

Check the scale carefully.

Make a small cross when you plot each point.

When you draw a curve on a graph, try to draw it without lifting your pencil off the paper.

The curve may not go exactly through all the points. If there are a few points above the curve, there should also be a few points below the curve.

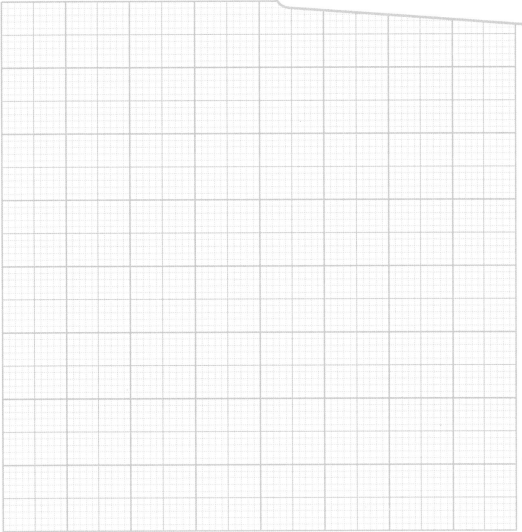

3 Is Jon and Anna's **prediction** correct? ………………………………

How do you know this?

………………………………………………………………………………………………

………………………………………………………………………………………………

4 How could they check these results are **reliable**?

………………………………………………………………………………………………

7.1 Elements on Earth

This exercise relates to **7.2 Atoms and elements** from the Coursebook.

> In this exercise, you practise presenting information in a bar chart.

1 The table shows the common elements in the crust of the Earth.

Present the information below as a **bar chart**.

Element	Percentage of Earth's crust
oxygen	47%
silicon	28%
aluminium	8%
iron	4.5%
calcium	3.5%
others	9%

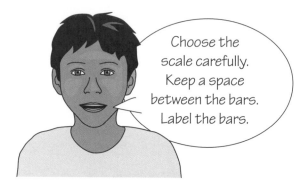

Choose the scale carefully. Keep a space between the bars. Label the bars.

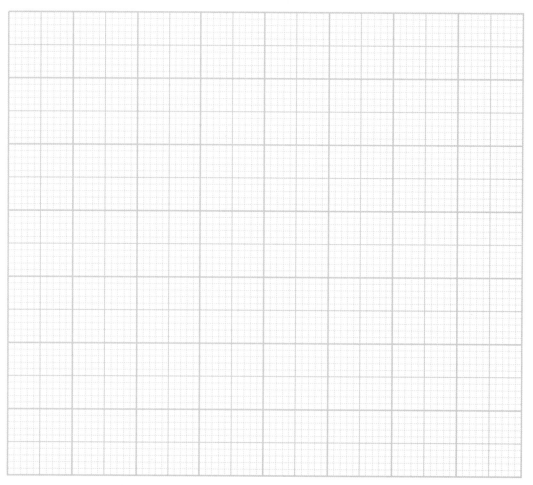

7.2 Using the Periodic Table

This exercise relates to **7.3 The Periodic Table** from the Coursebook.

In this exercise, you practise using the Periodic Table.

Scientists have organised all the elements into the Periodic Table.

The elements are arranged in order of the mass of their atoms.

The atoms with the smallest mass come first.

																	He helium
Li lithium	Be beryllium											B boron	C carbon	N nitrogen	O oxygen	F fluorine	Ne neon
Na sodium	Mg magnesium											Al aluminium	Si silicon	P phosphorus	S sulfur	Cl chlorine	Ar argon
K potassium	Ca calcium																

H
hydrogen

Part of the Periodic Table

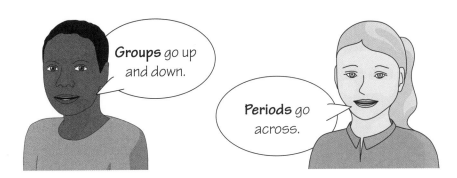

Groups go up and down.

Periods go across.

1 Are metal elements on the left or the right of the Periodic Table? ....

2 Name an element in the same group as boron. ....

3 Name an element in the same group as calcium. ....

4 Name an element in the same period as argon. ....

5 Name a gas in the same period as carbon. ....

7.3 True or false?

This exercise relates to **7.1 Atoms**, **7.2 Atoms and elements** and **7.4 Compounds** from the Coursebook.

> In this exercise, you decide if facts about atoms, molecules, elements and compounds are true or false.

Write **true** or **false** next to these statements.

1 Elements are made of only one type of atom. ....

2 Molecules are always made of different types of atoms. ....

3 Oxygen is a compound. ....

4 Calcium is an element. ....

5 Water is an element. ....

6

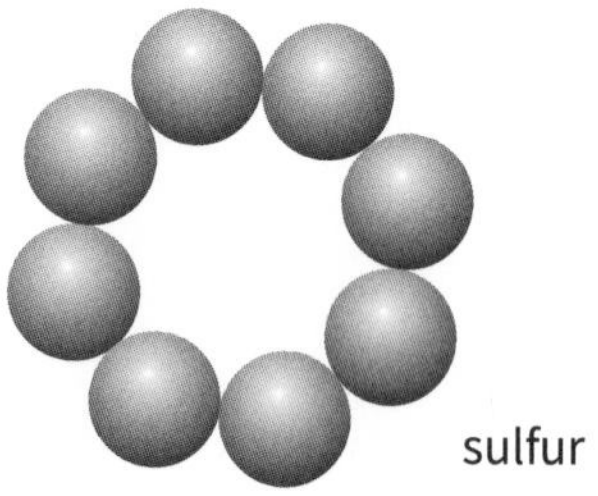

sulfur

The diagram above shows a molecule of sulfur. ....

7

neon

The diagram above shows molecules of neon. ....

8 A compound is made up of more than one type of atom. ....

7.4 Naming compounds

This exercise relates to **7.4 Compounds** from the Coursebook.

> In this exercise, you answer questions about the names of elements and compounds.

Compounds are made up of two or more different elements.

The name of the compound can tell you which elements are in it.

> **Look at these examples.**
>
> The compound **calcium oxide** contains calcium and oxygen.
>
> Sodium and chlorine form a compound called **sodium chloride**.

1 Which elements are in potassium chloride?

....

2 Which is the metal element in potassium chloride?

....

> **Remember**
>
> In the name of a compound containing a metal, the metal name goes first.

3 Which elements are in magnesium oxide?

....

4 Suggest the name of the compound that contains copper and oxygen.

....

5 Suggest the name of the compound that contains iron and chlorine.

....

> **Remember**
>
> When two elements combine, the compound name often ends in 'ide'.

7.5 Understanding formulae

This exercise relates to **7.5 Formulae** from the Coursebook.

> In this exercise, you answer questions about formulae of compounds.

Every compound has a formula. This is a short way of writing it.

The formula contains the symbols of the elements that are in the compound.

Look at this example.

The compound formed from sodium (symbol **Na**) and chlorine (symbol **Cl**) is sodium chloride. The formula of sodium chloride is

$$NaCl$$

Sodium chloride, NaCl, has **one** atom of sodium (Na) bonded with **one** atom of chlorine (Cl).

1 Complete this sentence.

Calcium oxide, CaO, has one atom of calcium bonded with ....

....

Now look at this example.

Some formulae have a small number next to a symbol. The number tells you how many atoms there are.

Water is a compound. Its formula is

$$H_2O$$

It has **two** atoms of hydrogen (H) bonded with **one** atom of oxygen (O).

2 Complete this sentence.

Sodium oxide, Na_2O, has ....

....

Remember

No number by a symbol means **one** atom of that element.

3 This diagram shows a molecule of hydrogen sulfide.

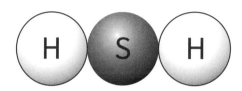

Write the formula. ....

4 This diagram shows a molecule of the compound methane.

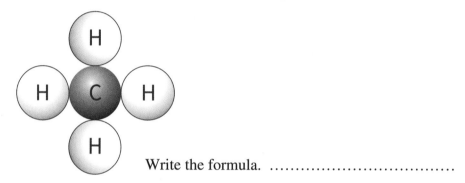

Write the formula. ....

5 Some of these are formulae of **compounds** and some are formulae of **elements**.

O_2 Na   MgO $CaCO_3$ H_2 Ar K_2O Li

Sort them out.

Compounds:

....

Elements:

....

....

Elements are made of only one type of atom.

8.1 Mixture or compound?

This exercise relates to **8.1 Compounds and mixtures** and **8.2 More about mixtures** from the Coursebook.

> In this exercise, you identify differences between mixtures and compounds.

In a compound, two or more elements are bonded together to make a new product.

In a mixture, two or more substances are mixed together, but they do **not** form a new product.

Amal mixes iron filings and sulfur in a beaker.

He stirs until the two substances are completely mixed.

Anna heats iron filings and sulfur powder together.

1 Tick **all** the correct statements.

   a Anna produces a new product. ☐

   b Amal produces a new product. ☐

   c Iron is magnetic. ☐

   d Something in Amal's beaker is attracted to a magnet. ☐

   e At the end of Anna's experiment, something in Anna's test tube is attracted to a magnet. ☐

f Anna's test tube contains a compound.

g Amal's beaker contains a compound.

h The atoms in Amal's beaker look like this.

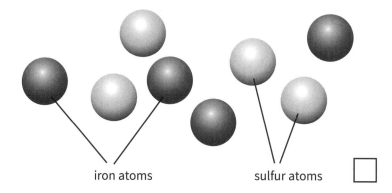

iron atoms   sulfur atoms

i The atoms in Anna's beaker look like this.

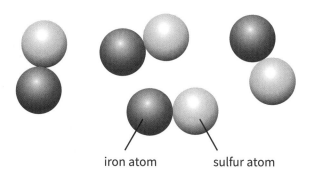

iron atom   sulfur atom

j Compounds have the same properties as the elements they are made from.

8.2 Choosing equipment

This exercise relates to **8.3 Separating mixtures** from the Coursebook.

> In this exercise, you choose equipment for a practical task and show how to use it. You also think about keeping safe when doing practical work.

Elsa has a mixture of sand, salt and water, in a beaker.
She wants to separate the sand, salt and water.

1 List all the pieces of equipment that Elsa will need.

Choose from the equipment shown here.

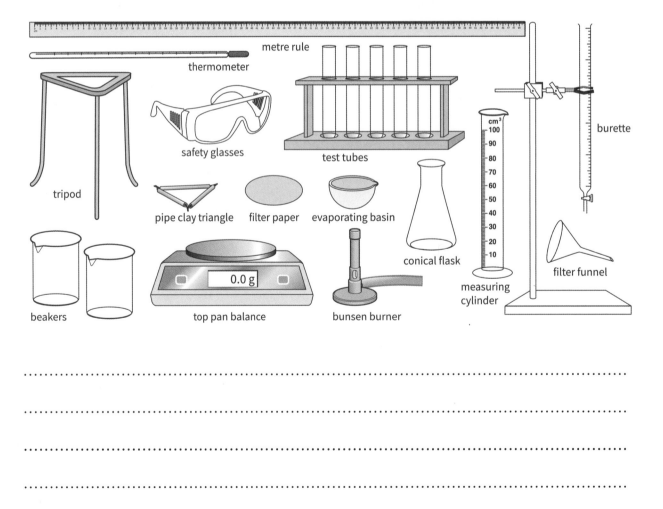

....

....

....

....

....

2 Show how to use your chosen equipment to separate out the sand. Draw and label a diagram.

3 Show how to use your chosen equipment to separate out the salt. Draw and label a diagram.

4 State one thing that Elsa must do to stay safe when she does this task.

....

....

8.3 Dissolving salt

This exercise relates to **8.7 Solubility investigation** from the Coursebook.

In this exercise, you interpret a graph of results and spot incorrect results.

Sam and Anna are investigating how much salt they can dissolve in different volumes of water.

The volume of the water they use is the **independent variable**.

This is what they do:

- Anna measures out the volume of water.

- Sam adds salt, one spatula at a time, until no more dissolves.

- He measures the mass of salt added.

If we use more water, I think more salt will dissolve.

This is the table of their results.

Volume of water in cm^3	Mass of salt in g
10	4
20	9
30	13
40	16
50	20
60	26
70	26
80	30
90	32
100	36

Sam plots this graph from their results.

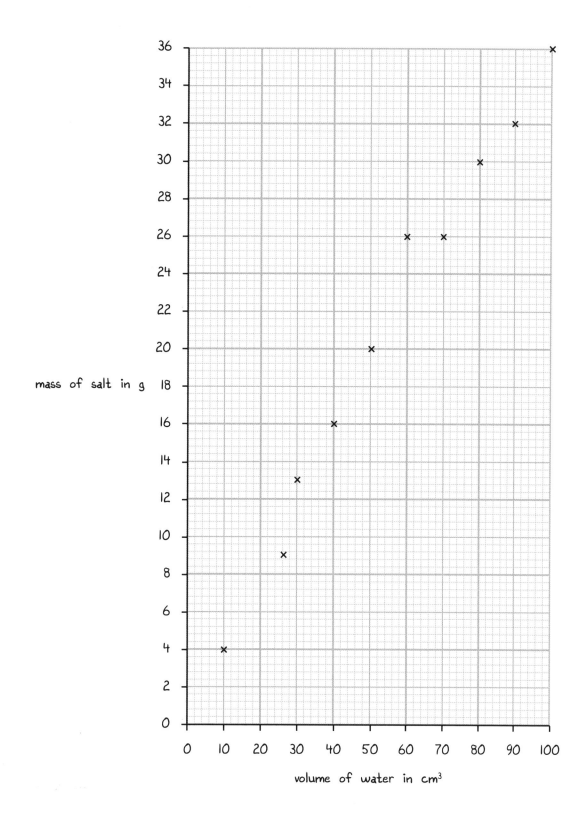

1 Which reading is plotted incorrectly? Draw a **red** circle around it on the graph.

2 Plot the point correctly on the graph.

3 Which other plotted point does not fit the pattern of the graph?
Draw a **blue** circle around this mass reading in the table, and around
the point on the graph.

4 Draw a **line of best fit** on the graph.

Remember

Draw a straight line with a ruler that follows the pattern of the points.

A line of best fit does not go through every point.

Ignore the points you have circled.

5 Describe what the graph shows.

....

....

Unit 9 Material changes

9.1 Physical or chemical?

This exercise relates to **9.1 Physical and chemical changes** from the Coursebook.

> In this exercise, you identify physical and chemical changes.

1 Tick **all** the correct statements.

In a physical change, no new substances are formed. ☐

When iron atoms bond with sulfur atoms, it is a chemical change. ☐

When ice melts to form water, it is a chemical change. ☐

When your cells use food to release energy, it is a physical change. ☐

When you cook an egg, it is a chemical change. ☐

When you let off fireworks, it is a physical change. ☐

2 In the chemical change shown here, oxygen reacts with hydrogen to form water.

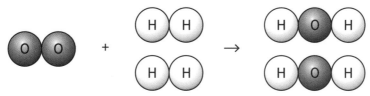

a Write the **word equation** for this reaction.

....

b The compound that is made in this reaction is ....

c The elements that make this compound are ....

9.2 Writing word equations

This exercise relates to **9.2 Burning** and **9.3 Reactions with acids** from the Coursebook.

> In this exercise, you practise writing word equations.

Remember

In a compound with a metal, the metal goes first in the name.

The name of the non-metal changes.

If two elements combine, the ending is often 'ide'.

If three elements that include oxygen combine, the ending is 'ate'.

When chemicals react together, we can show what happens by writing a word equation.

$$\text{magnesium} + \text{oxygen} \rightarrow \text{magnesium oxide}$$

Magnesium and oxygen are the **reactants** (the chemicals you start with). These go on the **left** of the equation.

Magnesium oxide is the **product**. This goes on the **right** of the word equation.

1 Write the word equation for the reaction between iron and sulfur.

....

2 Complete this word equation for the reaction between magnesium and hydrochloric acid.

magnesium + hydrochloric → .... + hydrogen
                       acid

3 In the space below, write the word equation for the reaction between zinc and hydrochloric acid.

Remember

Always write a word equation on one line.

If you need to, write long names like this

hydrochloric
acid

so that the equation fits on one line.

4 Complete this word equation for the reaction between a metal and sulfuric acid.

.... + sulfuric acid → magnesium sulfate + hydrogen

9.3 What happens to the atoms when chemicals react?

This exercise relates to **9.4 Rearranging atoms** from the Coursebook.

> In this exercise, you develop your understanding of how atoms rearrange in a chemical reaction.

When chemicals react together, none of the atoms is lost. They rearrange to make other chemicals.

1 In forming magnesium oxide, one atom of magnesium bonds with one atom of oxygen.

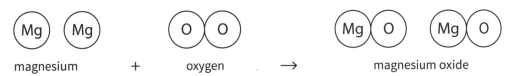

magnesium   +   oxygen   →   magnesium oxide

Colour the atoms of magnesium green. Colour the atoms of oxygen red.

2 This diagram shows magnesium and hydrochloric acid reacting.

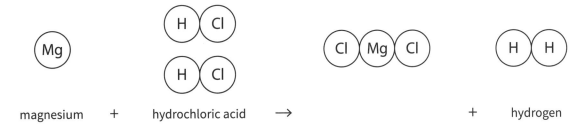

magnesium   +   hydrochloric acid   →   +   hydrogen

    a Colour the atoms of magnesium green. Colour the atoms of chlorine yellow. Leave the hydrogen atoms blank.

    b Name the compound that is produced.

    ....

3 a In the reaction shown in question 2, how many:

    atoms of hydrogen are on the left side of the equation? ....

    atoms of hydrogen are on the right side of the equation? ....

    atoms of chlorine are on the left side of the equation? ....

    atoms of chlorine are on the right side of the equation? ....

b Are there the same number of magnesium atoms on each side of the equation?

....

4 Now look at this reaction.

oxygen   +   hydrogen   →   water

a Colour the atoms of oxygen red. Leave the hydrogen atoms blank.

b Draw a circle around the word or words to make this statement correct:

The number of hydrogen atoms in the reactants is **larger / smaller /**

the same as the number of hydrogen atoms in the products.

c Write a statement about the number of oxygen atoms in the reactants and in the products.

....

....

....

9.4 What happens to the mass in a chemical reaction?

This exercise relates to **9.4 Rearranging atoms** and **9.5 More about conservation of mass** from the Coursebook.

> In this exercise, you work out the mass of the products in a reaction. You also explain some unexpected results.

Jon places 10 g of iron filings in a test tube. He adds 6 g of sulfur and mixes the two powders. He then heats the mixture.

The iron and sulfur react together to form iron sulfide.

When the reaction is complete the mass of the product is 16 g. The mass **does not change**.

iron and sulfur

Anna puts 15 g of iron filings and 9 g of sulfur in her test tube and heats it.

1 What is the mass of her product? .... g

2 Anna now adds 30 g of calcium carbonate to 50 g of hydrochloric acid.

What does Anna expect the reading on the balance to be when the reaction has finished?

....

Anna's reaction

hydrochloric acid

calcium carbonate

????

3 Anna notices that the reading on her balance is lower than she expects.

Explain why this is.

....

....

Remember

No mass is lost in a reaction.

Unit 10 Measuring motion

10.1 Speed

This exercise relates to **10.1 How fast? – Measuring speed** from the Coursebook.

> In this exercise, you develop your understanding of speed. Then you practise working out speed.

Speed is a way of describing how fast, or slow, something is moving.

To find the speed, you need to know two things:

- the distance (how far the object or person moves)

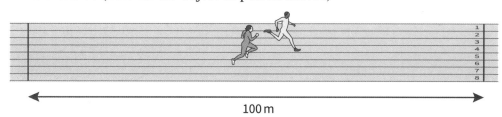

100 m

- the time (how many seconds, minutes or hours it takes to go that distance).

$$\text{speed} = \frac{\text{distance}}{\text{time}}$$

We sometimes write this as **average speed** for the whole journey, because the speed of an object can change during a journey.

Look at this example.

A train travels between two stations that are 250 km apart. It takes 5 hours. What is the average speed of the train in km/h?

Step 1 Find the distance. It is 250 km.

Step 2 Find the time. It is 5 hours.

Step 3 Divide 250 by 5.

$$\frac{250}{5} = 50$$

Step 4 Write the unit after the answer. Here the unit is given in the question as km/h, so the answer is 50 km/h.

> **Remember**
>
> To work out speed you **always** work out distance ÷ time.
>
> You do **not always** divide a bigger number by a smaller number.

1 Elsa runs 100 m.

She takes 20 s.

Work out Elsa's average speed in m/s.

....

2 Sam goes to his friend's house by bike.

His friend's house is 350 m away.

The journey takes 50 s.

Work out Sam's average speed in m/s.

....

3 An aeroplane flies between two airports that are 1500 km apart.

The flight takes 2 hours.

Work out the average speed of the aeroplane in km/h.

....

10.2 Units of speed

This exercise relates to **10.1 How fast? – Measuring speed** from the Coursebook.

> In this exercise, you practise using different units of speed.

The units of speed include:

m/s   **cm/s**   **km/h**

This speedometer shows the speed of a car. The speed of this car is 19 km/h

When you work out speed, you find the unit from the question.

Units will be given for distance and time. These give you the unit for speed.

Look at the pattern in the table.

Unit of distance	Unit of time	Unit of speed
centimetres, cm	seconds, s	centimetres per second, cm/s
metres, m	seconds, s	metres per second, m/s
kilometres, km	hours, h	kilometres per hour, km/h

1 Nor walks a distance of 50 m to the shops. It takes her 25 s.

Work out Nor's average speed.

Show your working **and** give the unit.

....

2 A ball rolls a distance of 87 cm down a ramp. It takes 29 s.

Work out the average speed of the ball.

Show your working **and** give the unit.

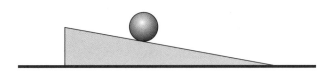

....

3 A ship travels a distance of 300 km in 10 hours.

Work out the average speed of the ship.

Show your working **and** give the unit.

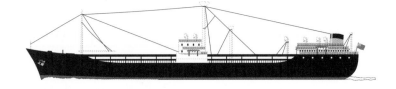

....

4 A tortoise walks a distance of 2 m in a time of 25 s.

Work out the average speed of the tortoise.

Show your working **and** give the unit.

> **Remember**
>
> Divide distance by time.
>
> You may need to divide a smaller number by a bigger number.

....

10.3 Another way to describe speed

This exercise relates to **10.5 Distance/time graphs** from the Coursebook.

> In this exercise, you interpret distance/time graphs.

Graphs can be used as pictures that describe how things change.

They are useful when it is too complicated to describe the change in words.

The graph here is called a **distance/time graph**.

It shows how the distance travelled by a train changes with time.

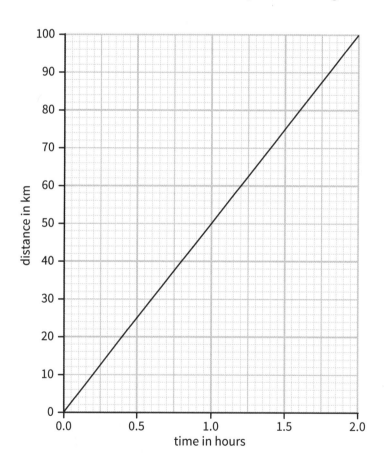

From the graph we can see:

- the line has a **constant slope** – this means the speed is constant

- the line goes up to 100 km (read from the vertical axis) and 2 hours (read from the horizontal axis) – this means the train has gone 100 km in 2 hours.

1 Use the information above to work out the speed of the train.

   Show your working **and** give the unit.

   ....

Look at the next distance/time graph.

- Between **A** and **B** on the graph, the object moves for 40 seconds.

- Between **A** and **B** on the graph, it moves a distance of 45 m.

- Between **B** and **C** on the graph, it is stopped (not moving) for 20 seconds.

- Between **C** and **D** on the graph, it is moving more slowly than between **A** and **B**.

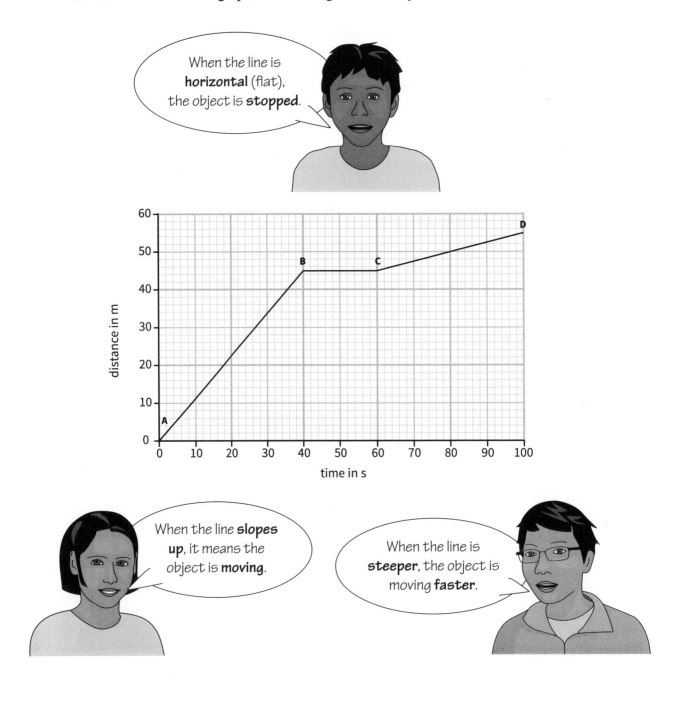

10 Measuring motion

Use the graph opposite to answer these questions.

2 What distance does the object move between **C** and **D**?

Give the unit.

....

3 How much time does it take the object to move between **C** and **D**?

Give the unit.

....

4 Work out the speed of the object between **C** and **D**.

Show your working **and** give the unit.

....

....

....

5 Why are graphs like the one opposite better for showing such a journey than a description in words?

List as many reasons as you can.

....

....

....

....

....

11.1 What makes sound?

This exercise relates to **11.1 Changing sounds** and **11.2 Looking at vibrations** from the Coursebook.

> **Remember**
>
> Sounds are made when things vibrate.

> In this exercise, you describe how sounds are different.

Sounds are caused by vibration. Sounds can be loud 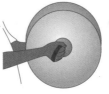 or quiet.

Loudness is caused by the **amplitude** of the vibration.

The louder the sound, the bigger the amplitude of vibration.

Sounds can have high pitch  or low pitch.

Pitch is caused by the **frequency** of the vibration.

The higher the pitch of the sound, the higher the frequency of vibration.

1 Draw a straight line from each description of sound to the property of the vibration that causes the sound.

description of sound   property of vibration

| pitch |

| amplitude |

| loudness |

| frequency |

2 Nor plays notes of different pitch on the piano. The notes are all the same loudness.

Complete the sentences.

Choose words from this list:

gets higher

gets lower

stays the same

a As the pitch of the note gets higher, the frequency of the sound ....

b The amplitude of the notes she plays ....

3 Nor now hits a drum.

When she hits the drum harder, it makes a louder sound.

What happens to the amplitude of the vibration as the sound gets louder?

....

11.2 Looking at sound waves

This exercise relates to **11.4 Sounds on a screen** from the Coursebook.

In this exercise, you compare sound waves.

Sound is carried by sound **waves**.

Sound waves can be picked up by a microphone.

The sound wave can then be shown on equipment called an **oscilloscope**.

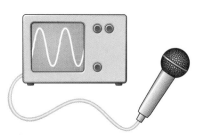 

1   Look at the two sound waves **A** and **B**.

A    **B**

   a   When the sound changes from **A** to **B**, what happens to the **amplitude** of the wave?
   Tick **one** box.

   increases

   decreases

   stays the same

   b   When the sound changes from **A** to **B**, what happens to the **loudness** of the sound?
   Tick **one** box.

   increases

   decreases

   stays the same

2 Look at the two sound waves **X** and **Y**.

X

Y

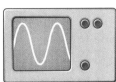

a When the sound changes from **X** to **Y**, what happens to the **pitch** of the sound?
   Tick **one** box.

   increases ☐

   decreases ☐

   stays the same ☐

b When the sound changes from **X** to **Y**, what happens to the **loudness** of the sound?
   Tick **one** box.

   increases ☐

   decreases ☐

   stays the same ☐

c When the sound changes from **X** to **Y**, what happens to the **frequency** of the wave?
   Tick **one** box.

   increases ☐

   decreases ☐

   stays the same ☐

12.1 Light rays

This exercise relates to **12.1 How light travels** and **12.2 How shadows form** from the Coursebook.

> In this exercise, you practise drawing light rays.

Light travels in straight lines called light rays.

Nor has three cards with holes in the middle. She supports the cards with modelling clay.

She makes sure the holes are in a straight line.

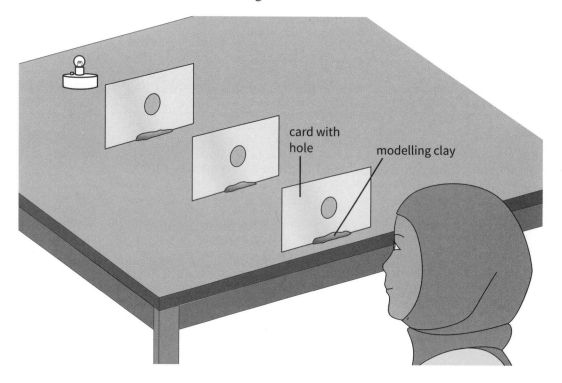

card with hole

modelling clay

1 Nor looks at a lamp though the holes.

Draw the light ray from the lamp to Nor.

> **Remember**
>
> Use a ruler when you draw the light ray.
>
> Draw an arrow on the light ray to show its direction.

Nor then moves the middle card so the hole is **not** in line with the other two holes.

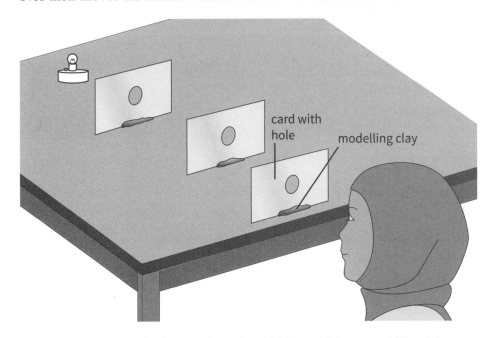

2 She **cannot** see the lamp when the middle card is moved like this.

Explain this.

....

....

Elsa has a piece of transparent plastic and a piece of opaque card.

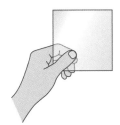 

> **Remember**
>
> Transparent means light **can** pass through.
>
> Opaque means light **cannot** pass through.

She puts the transparent plastic and the opaque card between herself and a lamp.

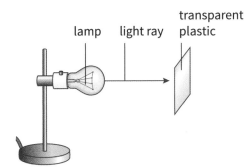 

lamp   light ray   transparent plastic   opaque card

3 Elsa **cannot** see the lamp.

Draw the light ray on the diagram to show its path. It has been started for you.

12.2 Light and shadows

This exercise relates to **12.2 How shadows form** from the Coursebook.

> In this exercise, you predict the position of a shadow.
> You also describe variables in an investigation.

Sam has a piece of opaque card and a lamp.

He uses the card to make a shadow on the wall. His set-up is shown in the diagram.

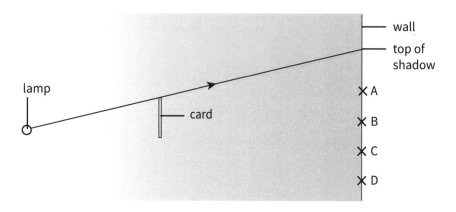

The diagram shows one light ray from the lamp.

This light ray meets the wall at the **top** of the shadow.

1 At which point on the wall is the **bottom** of the shadow?

Draw a circle around **one** letter.

    A   **B**   **C**   **D**

> **Remember**
>
> A shadow forms when an
> opaque object blocks light rays.

Sam measures the height of the shadow from top to bottom.

He wants to find out how the shadow's height changes when he moves the card towards or away from the wall.

2 Sam needs to measure the distance between the card and the wall.

What can he use to do this?

....

....

3 What is the **independent variable** in Sam's investigation?

....

....

4 What is the **dependent variable**?

....

5 State **two** variables that Sam must keep the same.

1 ....

....

2 ....

....

> **Remember**
>
> Sam is investigating how the height of the shadow **depends on** the distance between the card and the wall.

12.3 Reflection from a non-luminous object

This exercise relates to **12.3 How reflections form** from the Coursebook.

> In this exercise, you draw light rays reflecting off non-luminous objects.

Non-luminous objects do **not** give out light. We see
them when light reflects off them, into our eyes.

1 Amal is reading a book in his room.

The only source of light in the room is a ceiling lamp.

> **Remember**
>
> Light travels **away** from a light source.
>
> Light reflecting off objects travels
> **towards** our eyes.

Draw the light rays that allow Amal to see the book.

Show the direction of the light rays.

Jupiter ◯

2 This diagram shows the Sun,
Jupiter and Earth.

The Sun gives out light. Jupiter
does **not** give out its own light.

Draw the light rays that allow
Jupiter to be seen from Earth.

not to scale

Show the direction of the light rays.

Earth ○

Sun

12.4 Reflection from a mirror

This exercise relates to **12.3 How reflections form** from the Coursebook.

In this exercise, you draw light rays reflecting from mirrors, and measure angles. You need a protractor.

Look at the light ray coming to the mirror.

Jon explains how to draw the reflected ray.

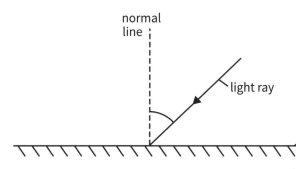

1 Measure the angle between the light ray and the normal line.

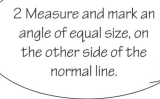

2 Measure and mark an angle of equal size, on the other side of the normal line.

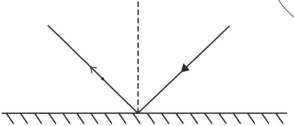

3 Use a ruler to draw a light ray at this angle. Draw an arrow to show the ray is coming from the mirror.

Remember

Make sure the light ray that you draw touches:

- the end of the other light ray
- the end of the normal line
- the mirror.

In this diagram a ray of light hits a mirror.

The **angle of incidence** has been measured for you. This is labelled **I**.

1 Draw the reflected ray on the diagram. To help you, read Jon's steps on the previous page.

Label the **angle of reflection** with an **R**.

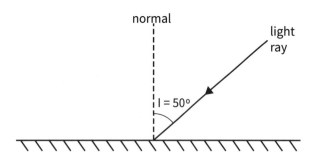

2 What is the value of your angle **R**?

R = ...

3 Measure the angle of incidence on the diagram below.

Write its value on the diagram.

4 Draw the reflected ray on the diagram.

Write the value of the angle of reflection on the diagram.

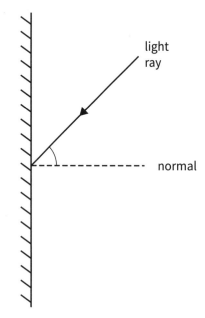

12.5 Looking at coloured objects

This exercise relates to **12.6 Coloured light** from the Coursebook.

> In this exercise, you predict which colours of light are reflected from, or absorbed by, coloured objects.

When we look at a non-luminous coloured object, we see the colour of light that the object reflects.

Other colours of light are absorbed by the object.

Nor is in a room with a white light. She looks at a blue cup.

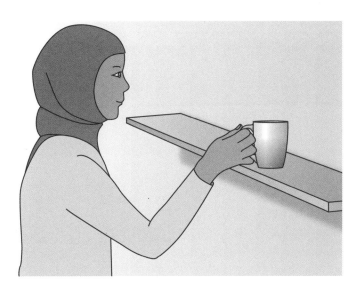

> ### Remember
>
> The colours of the spectrum of white light are:
>
> **red, orange, yellow, green, blue, indigo, violet.**

1 Which colour of light is **reflected** from the blue cup?
Tick **one** box.

red ☐   yellow ☐

orange ☐   blue ☐

2 Which colours of light are **absorbed** by the blue cup?
Tick **all** correct boxes.

white ☐   red ☐   orange ☐   yellow ☐

green ☐   blue ☐   indigo ☐   violet ☐

3 Nor switches off the white light in the room.

She switches on a green light.

What colour will the blue cup appear to be in the green light?

white ☐   green ☐   blue ☐   black ☐

4 Explain your answer to question 3.

....

....

....

Unit 13 Magnetism

13.1 Which materials are magnetic?

This exercise relates to **13.1 Magnets and magnetic materials** from the Coursebook.

> In this exercise, you draw a table, then sort objects into those that are magnetic and those that are not.

Only some materials are magnetic.

Iron is the most common magnetic metal.

Steel contains iron mixed with other elements. Most types of steel are magnetic.

Other common metals, such as copper and aluminium, are **not** magnetic.

Non-metals, such as plastic, wood and paper, are **not** magnetic.

1 Draw a table beside the pictures to sort the objects into those that are **magnetic** and those that are **not magnetic**.

Remember

Draw your table with a pencil and a ruler.

Write a heading for each column.

Include the names of **all** the objects from the pictures.

iron nail

aluminium drink can

copper wire

wooden toy

plastic comb

iron gate

13.2 Rules about magnets

This exercise relates to **13.2 Magnetic poles** from the Coursebook.

> In this exercise, you predict what will happen when two magnets are brought together.

Every magnet has two **poles**. The poles are at opposite ends, or sometimes at opposite sides, of the magnet.

The poles are called **north**, or **N**, and **south**, or **S**.

The rules about magnets are:

Two poles that are different will attract each other.

Two poles that are the same will repel each other.

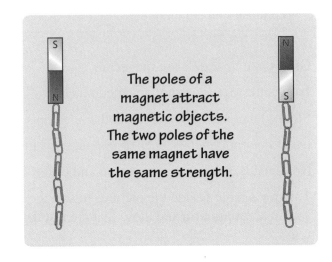

The poles of a magnet attract magnetic objects. The two poles of the same magnet have the same strength.

1 Beside each pair of magnets, write the word **attract** or the word **repel** to predict what will happen.

> **Remember**
>
> 'Repel' is the opposite of 'attract'. It means to push away.

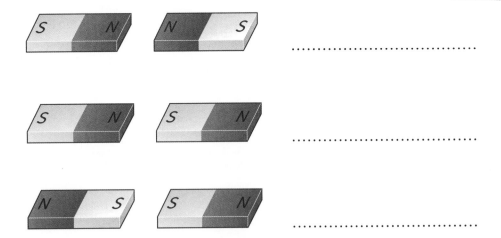

....

....

....

A horseshoe magnet is like a bar magnet that is bent into a curved shape.

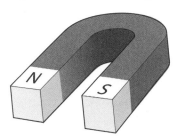

Elsa has a horseshoe magnet.

She does not know which pole is which.

Elsa also has a bar magnet with the poles correctly marked.

2 Describe how Elsa can use her bar magnet to discover which pole is which on her horseshoe magnet.

Elsa can: ....

....

She will see: ....

....

13.3 Drawing a magnetic field pattern

This exercise relates to **13.3 Magnetic field patterns** from the Coursebook.

> In this exercise, you draw the magnetic field pattern around a bar magnet.

When you move a magnetic object away from a magnet, the attraction gets weaker.

When the object is far enough away, it will not be attracted at all.

The area around the magnet where magnetic objects are attracted is called the **magnetic field**.

We cannot see a magnetic field, but we can draw the pattern like this:

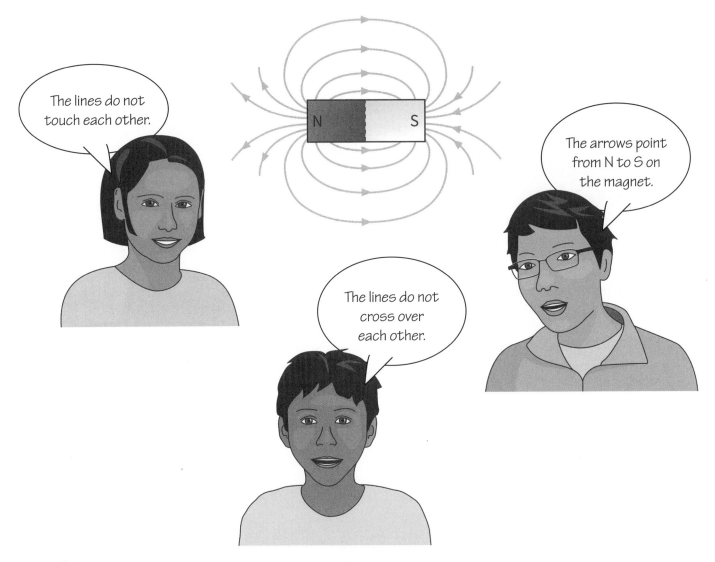

The lines do not touch each other.

The lines do not cross over each other.

The arrows point from N to S on the magnet.

1 Copy the magnetic field pattern from the diagram opposite onto this bar magnet.

2 Draw the magnetic field around this magnet.

Remember

Check which way round the poles are **before** you add any arrows.

13.4 Testing an electromagnet

This exercise relates to **13.4 Making an electromagnet** and **13.5 A stronger electromagnet** from the Coursebook.

> In this exercise, you decide on variables to keep the same in an investigation, and look for results that do not fit a pattern.

Sam makes an electromagnet.

He coils a wire around a big iron nail.

He connects the ends of the wire to a battery.

Sam uses his electromagnet to pick up paper clips.

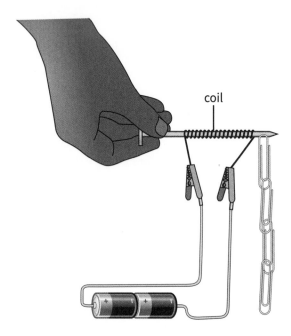

coil

Sam then changes the number of coils of wire around the nail. He wants to answer the question:

How does the number of coils affect the strength of the electromagnet?

Each time he changes the number of coils, he counts the number of paper clips his electromagnet will lift.

1 Write down **two** other things that Sam should keep the same.

....

....

The table shows Sam's results.

Number of coils	Number of paper clips lifted
10	2
20	4
30	4
40	8
50	10

2 Draw a circle around the **anomalous** result in the table.

3 How can Sam check his results to confirm this one was anomalous?

> **Remember**
>
> **Anomalous** means that it does not fit the pattern.

....

4 Sam makes a **conclusion** from his results.

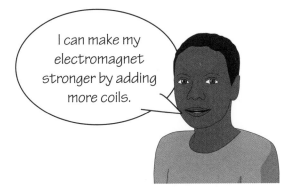

I can make my electromagnet stronger by adding more coils.

Write down **one other** way that he could make his electromagnet stronger.

....

....